laden with rust

paige maskell

i am made of sparking wires
and rusted metal.
inside my walls are broken gears
and unfinished ideas
that grind away at my steel heart.
i can switch off my mind at will
   (i do so a lot).
my springs hold me up
enough to give the illusion
that my programming functions
   (but it doesn't).

for pluto

part one: rust

my lungs are filled with toxins
but they no longer sting.
      i welcome them in
      like old friends;
i invite them to dance.
they stay in my frame
as welcome guests,
despite the havoc they wreak
on my tired, weakened mind.
      i let them stay,
      for while they are here
      at least i feel something.

my limbs quiver,
softly under the heavy
fabrics i keep draped
over my body.
the numbness starts
in the depths of my
brain, and i feel it slither
through my veins and
fill my lungs. it forms
a solid stone under
my heart and makes
everything feel like
the earth is pulling me
into its core. why does
nothing feel real? i
think i'm made of
whispers and worries,
the things that have
been plaguing my thoughts
since the day i realized
that other people's opinions
mean more to me than
how i feel about myself.
i can't stop picturing
myself in another life, as
another girl who doesn't
deal with quivering limbs,
a girl who isn't made of
whispers are worries.

of course i'm a fan
of self-deprecation
how else can we laugh
at the pathetic ways we
change to please society

you tore my heart to shreds,
you left the pieces on my kitchen floor.
it was too poignant a mess to fix alone,
but lord knows i wouldn't let you close to me again.
i spent years bearing bruises
that should never have seen light.
you left me grieving and mangled,
matted hair stuck to salty cheek.
what old wounds do you seek to open?
humour me.

it's strange to realize that on our
crowded earth i am entirely alone;
just a lunatic and the moon in the sky.

the stars whisper to me at night.
you would be surprised by their words.
instead of promises of tomorrow,
they breathe songs that run up my spine
and attach themselves inside of my skull,
slowly tearing me apart.
they murmur anxieties
that pulse through my veins
and stale the air in my lungs.
the stars are my constant tormentors,
reminders of woe to come.

there are things in life
that tug at your soul
and make your heart
rupture, and those are
the things that cannot
        be held on to. beauty
        like that smolders like fire,
        and you still struggle
        to allow yourself to burn.

i want to rip into the
core of my body.
i want to watch my
flesh boil off my
frame; watch it swirl
in the sink, away from
the mangled new owner
of a pair of fresh, gleaming
scars that exist to remind
her of the constant struggle
against herself. i find myself
compelled by the pain, i
find trust in the feeling that
i know is always one little slip
away.

i don't want you
to feel responsible
for me and yet
every time i fall
apart i find myself
back in your arms
asking you to fix me
and i don't know
how to love myself,
yet somehow you
manage to love me
so well and i'm sorry
that you feel like i
am your problem.

my limbs are heavy with the weight of the burden
        that my body endures as it listens to my mind.
        or perhaps it is the earth tugging me into her core,
willing my return to the deepest parts of her body.
regardless, the feeling is exquisitely agonizing,
suggesting the transience of my existence.

every crack in my lips i find filled with dust;
a fault of my own, on account of the
fact that i have not moved from
under my sheets in far too many hours.

my brain is made of static,
    my thoughts now come out foggy,
    and i don't know how
    to light my mind on fire
    the way it had been before.
every word that escapes my lips
bites the air with each syllable,
transforming into a bygone notion,
    lost to the wind.

close your eyes and
remember the time
your mother held you
tight despite you insisting
that you were too old for
her hugs. you let yourself
melt into her arms
anyways because
she is the only person
who has yet to hurt you.

something inside me is hurting.
maybe one day, i'll find out what.

i have been holding my breath
all afternoon
wondering if anyone would notice
the lack of air reaching my lungs
and the colour rising in my cheeks
but instead i find myself
alone on my bedroom floor
lightheaded and crushed
i don't know how to stop doing this to myself

vulnerable was never something i
thought i was.
i always tried to be strong, steadfast,
someone to admire
for being made of stiff concrete,
though lately i realize it's not con-
crete,
but a thin layer of plaster that i have
built around me.
it allows only the most faint touch
before it cracks,
which causes the entirety of my en-
casing to dissolve;
i realize that i must be held gingerly
or not at all.
i realize that i am more vulnerable
than i think.

i find it
inexplicably
hard to swallow
all of the hurt that
was forced down my throat;
an avalanche
rolling through my body,
across every surface,
around every bone that
breaks with each phantom
brush of your hand.

your hobby of tearing the skin off your bones
is the reason you feel like your thoughts
are tumbling out of you;
you're destroying yourself.

the most heartbreaking thing
i do to myself is that i
look back at things i can't change
and convince myself that if only i
had done more, or done better,
i would be somewhere wholly different.

some days
it feels like it's raining
everywhere.

it feels like gravity is willing me back
into the earth's core
because it knows that someone
as empty as myself cannot stand
to be on the surface of this planet
any longer.

it's like
a drill
forcing
its way
into the
center of
your chest,
grinding bone
and churning
organs until you
become a giant
human stew.
blood, flesh and
raw marrow seep
through the hole
that you find in
not only your
breastbone, but
through the very
back of your spine.
you start to see
static. your
eyelids grow heavy.

i could never explain
the extent to which it
hurts but let me tell you
it feels like a hurricane
ravaging my insides
until i am nothing
more than debris.

i think
i'm hovering
an inch off the ground
because every step i take
feels as though i'm not taking a step at all.
i feel disconnected from myself again.
every movement feels mechanic,
like i am not the one
in control of the actions that keep me alive.
i wonder, who is making sure i breathe and blink?
because i'm not doing anything of the sort.
i can't feel my hands but they're right in front of me.
there's an emptiness in my chest-
like a balloon, swelling inside a body
that doesn't feel like my own.
i keep asking, do i exist?
but that's a question i don't know how to answer.
i feel like my mind is stuck in an empty room.
i've been checking my pulse every minute for the past hour,
just to make sure that this isn't what it feels like to die.
how is it that everyone can continue
to live blindly when the world feels like
a simulation of reality?
i wish i knew,
because maybe then i wouldn't feel
like i stumbled out of my skin
and into a place where i don't belong.

the wind,
which usually drags us apart,
is now all that is holding us together.

i want you to explain to me
in thorough, painful detail
every moment that led you
to this decision.
i want to know what it was
that brought on the idea
of setting yourself free by
removing the dying parts of
your life
(and by that i mean
the one who can't get
it through her head that it's
over).

there is something blistering inside
you, i can see it. you keep finding
        yourself maimed, head between
your knees. i've watched you
    crumble. it breaks my heart
        to see a soul as astounding as
yours fall victim to your unsteady
                mind, time after time.

YOU ARE THE BURNING IN THE BACK OF MY THROAT
ON NIGHTS WHEN I AM LONELY BUT NOT QUITE ALONE
AND IT HURTS BUT GODDAMN I'M ADDICTED TO IT
THERE IS NOTHING I WANT MORE THAN TO FEEL YOU:
         THE BURNING IN THE BACK OF MY THROAT

my heart is heavy,
                  my lungs are arid and
i can't stand the
        feeling of so many voices
around me making
memories while all i do
          is sink further into
                      my skin.

i want you to take me
to the places you hate
the places where you feel something
and where honesty runs like rivers,
flowing down the steady incline
of a relationship that is slowly
collapsing my lungs and giving
a home to something that has
been growing inside me for far too long,
can you show me all of the things
that make your chest heave with anxiety
all the thoughts that leave your legs planted
in the damp earth of this lonely island
where we have left ourselves stranded.

i have wrapped myself
in caution tape.
bright yellow, it screams:
keep out, there is nothing
for you here.

hold my hand
please, your hands are
so warm compared to
mine - my body gave up on
my mind too long ago and
i have coagulated into
a mess almost as horrific
as the one going on in
my conscience.
now i have to rely on the
kindness of others and
it is so hard to find someone
willing to give a second of
their time to a cause that
reaps them no reward.

i'm lonely but i'm far from alone.
i hear the voices whispering,
behind rumpled curtains and in neglected corners.
i feel them run their fingers through my hair.
they hum refrains in my ear; they allege that they love me.

there are days i worry i can see them.

for the one
who won't come back
despite promises that you would:
will you at least return
my heart,
the one you dissolved with a touch
of your calloused fingers
which then found their way
to my shrinking wrist
and held me tight.
where will you go now
without me by your side,
i guess i'll find out
if we ever meet again.
can i return the
memories that find me
in the middle of the night,
the ones that steal my breath
and leave every limb
stinging with wist
that clings onto my breaking back
for days thereafter.
what happened to all of the things
you whispered in my ears on
days where i was loneliest;
what will come of the
moments where i realize that
i am isolated from not just
you but the fabric of reality?
tell me how i'm supposed to
deal with myself
without you here.

you always took things out of me
and never left anything in their place

i haven't washed my hair in weeks.
it's riddled with not just grease
but matted, dried blood from
all the clawing i have done to my skull
in an effort to extract thoughts
that still slither into my conscious.
i cannot express how badly
i want to let the scalding hot water
wash away the screams that echo through my hollow head
but i know that no matter how hard i try
there is nothing temporary about this state of mind
so why should my body be any less destroyed?

i have started to believe
that i don't really
exist as a person.
there really isn't anything
of which i am certain and
when i walk it's as if
my feet aren't even
touching the floor.
this body doesn't belong
to my mind anymore.

i didn't realize how fragile i was until
you dropped me and i shattered
like china on concrete,
every piece of me has turned to dust
that settled around my vulgar mess of a room
in which i have planted myself,
despite my hope to grow roots
in places much brighter than this

there is so much
inside me that
i don't know
how to show you;
things i don't
even know
how to show
myself.

it's hard to have been half of a whole for so long
and to suddenly be forced to hold yourself together
as that whole starts to rot around you
like a house crumbling from its base
at the slightest tilt of the earth.

you have made me feel
like there is fire inside me
that burns with every sensation imaginable
if only i could look in your eyes now,
and let you see in mine,
let you see what you made me feel.

        i want it to suffocate you. i want
        the pressure of what you have done
        to coil around your ribs,

                tighter until you forget
                what it means to breathe, because
                that is how you left me.

more than anything, i want to crawl back into the way i would feel
as your breath warmed the back of my neck and as feet brushed bare feet
under freshly washed, soap-smelling sheets and i want to be able to see you and have
a smile spread across my face but instead all i feel is a burning between my eyes
that grows into a shrill screaming echoing on my broken eardrums, further shattering
someone that is already shattered.

being free
weighs so much
on my shoulders.
i did not expect
something so beautiful
to be such a burden.

there is no love here.
sickness, maybe. but no love.
words like knives, digging
into overripe fields of emotion
on days that seemed as
unimportant as passing thoughts,
turned to crushing memories.
there is no longer a sense
of connection or passion or
willingness to be a constant
in a life full of changing variables.
i have realized that those feelings
evaporated long ago,
and in their place there had been
nothing more than
a skeleton of the person
who i thought i deserved.

washing off the memories is proving to be impossible
i find scraps of you under my nails
and pieces of you in my hair.
your smell is still under my skin
and the ghost of your lips still on mine,
reminding me that you are both
here and
gone, all at once.

if you ever
find words
to explain
the hurt,
send them
my way.

sometimes i'm floating on thoughts
that are held together by fraying string
                    came undone as the result
of heavy breathing meant to calm
the storm in my mind, the one
that brought on winds heavy enough
            to make me feel like i am weightless,
        as though i'm being carried through life
without ever having need
to touch the ground.

part two: polish

flowers only bloom in sunlight.
surround yourself with it.
bathe in effervescence,
it will make your skin glow
as you shower yourself in positivity
and let flowers grow in your mind.
brave this contemporary universe
by making something of the thoughts in your head.
you are bubbly and lustrous and radiant.
allow yourself to bloom.

i am a hoarder of morbid luxuries

and i desperately need to add you to my collection

i can't explain how
badly i want to climb
your mountainous mind.
the rocky cliffs that
shape the landscape of
your body are beautiful,
and yet i would rather learn
what it is that makes your
mind bud with nature
instead of how long it takes
to make the terrain of your
body quake with pleasure.

the earth under my feet is fickle
as i lean on your shoulder.
you are just as fickle as the ground beneath our feet
　　　　and the passing clouds in the sky.
it's as if your mind sees one thing
as mine finds another, and suddenly
we find ourselves on different sides of the universe.
　　　　　　　　why are you so far away?
and yet in the same moment,
here you are, right beside me.

the universe is calling me
she keeps shouting out my name.
her call echoes off the asteroids,
and i feel her pull me closer.
she embraces me with the milky way.
the stars shine in my hair,
creating shadows on my face
as if i am the dark side of the moon.
reach out and trace delicate fingers
over far more delicate planets.
smile at them and they might just smile back.

i want to be
the horizon line
and i want you
to be the sea,
our nautical lips
curved into smiles
as we kiss eternally.

villainizing yourself
when you have done no wrong
will only deepen your pain.

i would trade the sun to see you
because you are the only light i need.

charge me with your reality,
i want to bleed your truth.

hold my heartsick, glacial hands
and remind me how it is to feel whole.

free me from my trouble,
help me rediscover warmth in your arms.

i am enamored by the way
your words pick me up
as if i am lighter than air
and bring me to places that
i had stopped believing in
so many years ago.

her golden fingertips brush the waking dawn.
she sits with her guileless face to the sky,
slowly drinking in the hallowed morning air
and readying herself to grow another day.

you are a planet
that i have yet to explore.
i watch as flowers grow out your ears
and as your moonbeam fingers
trace stars on the back of my hand.
you make mountains fall flat
and rivers change their odious tune
to a lonely, blissful hum.
how do you break things with your will
and then repair them with your sickly sweet rhythm?
what is it that makes nature listen?
sing me the melody of the universe.
share with me her sorrow.

you are poison,
a river of acid coursing
through my splitting lips
and even though it stings
i can't help but beg for more.

flowers grow out of the tips of your fingers.
you are the soft morning light
pouring through half-shut blinds
and making them squint at your beauty.
remind the world that there is allure
in even the most insignificant.
show them how to inhale radiance,
and let the ineffable seep through their skin.
allow them to brush the hair out of your eyes,
let them see you standing there.
show them what it is to live unobstructedly.

you are more
than the love
you receive.

capture your

breath in jars

for the days you

find yourself

gasping for air.

we are a resilient force;
fervor spills from our ears.
our spirit is formed of radiant hope,
and it shines as a beacon
to the hopeless discontented.
take up arms, face the toxic empire.
hold your brave heads high.
scream at the world,
tell them who we are.

we are women.

can you tell me what it feels like
when someone loves you
entirely, wholly
for every nick and scar and freckle
and mole on your cheek?

because this is a feeling i have yet to experience.
it's as if someone has decided
that i am not worthy of feeling
entirely, wholly
encompassed by appreciation for who i have become.

i have so far to grow, of which i am
entirely, wholly
aware, and yet it would be a new feeling
to be recognized for how far i have come
and how far i am going to go.

loving you is like wailing into an empty void
without a hint of an echo.
i can't stand loving you.
it pulls me in every direction;
the sadness of it consumes me.
i am drained by the endeavors i make.
you lead my mind to wander
and i constantly return decorated in wounds.
you veil yourself with barbed wire
and refuse to let me trim your thorns.
i want to free you.

i find myself obsessing
over the infinity of the universe,
yet there is still so much magnificence
i have yet to uncover here on earth.

you have been
through so much pain
i'm so proud that you've held on.

dependence is both the most beautiful and the most destructive attribute observed within the human scale of emotion. the fact that there's something, or someone, that makes your life better to the point that being without it draws a feeling out of you that you've never felt before, like you threw loss and melancholy and grief into a blender and swallowed your sorrow smoothie whole. it breaks you, it rips you to the point of not being able to breathe. yet the same thing that brings you pain is what makes you laugh until you can feel every inch of your body fill with liquid joy. the most contradictory, unproductive feeling experienced by a conscious being on this earth and yet here we are searching for someone, something to depend on to make our lives feel like they're worth more than we originally imagined.

you need to
grab your life by the reins
and hold on tight
because your life is
going to be a long
and wild ride. but
it will be worth it
i promise you that
so please don't
ever let go.

i didn't know
what to do with you
so i made you into ink
and turned you into poetry

soft light falls
on your narrow shoulders,
your jagged edges draw
shadows across the floor,
the lace on your neck
leaves patterns on sheets
long stained with memories
of days that left too quickly.

i miss you, but not the way i used to.
i miss the glow of the sun bouncing
off your cheeks, but i remind myself
that despite the way you shone, you
were malevolent and unstable. you
were so insecure about your own
existence that you found ways to
claw at mine.
and yet, i miss the
stars that i saw in your eyes when
you talked about the things you loved,
like sundays and poetry and me. i miss
how your hands moved so quickly when you spoke
that it made my head spin, and how your
hair fell around your gentle shoulders.
i miss your silhouette as you stood
above me, urging me to do things
I never thought possible. it used to
be hard to picture a life without you.
now, it's my reality. i miss you,
but not in the way i used to.

you create ripples in my heart,
the same way the moon creates waves in the sea;
i'm a victim of your gravitational pull

i learned so much
in so little time
about how to brace yourself
as your body shuts down, as
wildfire crackles in your core
and scatters ashes across
your insides.
i learned that you cannot
allow your body to
take in more than is intended
and that sometimes the best
medicine is nothing at all.

it's nice to feel the butterflies.

i didn't think i'd be able to feel them again,
but here they are, filling me with a giddiness
i only experienced once before, with you.

never before have i met someone
with stars dancing in their eyes as
they talk about the things that shaped them,
and the things that made them better.
the experience of hearing your words
as they circle my mind is like no other;
i have truly felt something new with you.

grab the moon in your fist
use its glow to guide you,
if only for a night.

there was a moment
not too long ago
where we were pressed
against each other,
      skin to skin,
and i felt your heart race
in time with mine.
that was when it hit me
how badly i want you
to be by my side
for as long as
possible.

sometimes i stare directly into the sun.
i'm still quite not sure why,
but i convince myself that by doing so
i break rules set by the universe
long, long ago. it warms me
in the same way the sun warms
the surface of my face.

the walls of this hospital are a soft blue.

if you were a colour,
        you would be this colour.
the same shade as the sky
on a day that's not yet overcast.
like how your mind is sometimes
        clear, soon to be clouded.

these walls make me want to
    walk through the tall grass again
and lie down so that the blades
    look like they touch the clouds,
        the same way we did.

        if you were a memory,
    you would be that memory.

i know that
the woman i am becoming
is stronger than the girl i used to be.

you are incandescent;
nothing can hold you back
from emerging brighter.

you're the sweet tune
stuck in my head,
a melody that plays
in moments when my fingers
brush against yours.

and i can't stop dancing
to the sickly sweet song
that i found once i
touched you.

after i fell in love with the rain,
sunny days seemed dimmer
and sunsets had nothing on
frigid drops of water on my cheeks.
some nights the rain would serenade me,
letting me know there was someone
listening, watching, turning my thoughts
into music.

i fell in love with the rain on the day
i decided breathing was too hard,
and my feet carried me out into the
fresh air. the sky opened up and
i found myself both embraced and
numbed by the feeling of my dripping,
wet clothes clinging to my skin, and my
dripping, wet conscience clinging to
the sensation of being cold and soaked
and undoubtedly alive.

sometimes the only thing
that can keep you from tumbling
over the edge is yourself.

today the love
that i feel is platonic.
i no longer have to feel
pressure from the
intense, romantic love
that used to grasp
at my ankles
and drag me down.
the love around
me is no longer toxic;
the lovers i have
are those who hold me
as close as i hold them,
and i now know that
that is all i really need.

you touched me
like i was something sacred
and suddenly the world
felt a little more real.

go to a coffee shop at night
right before they close,
make them roll their eyes
at you for lengthening
their evening.
get a cup of the most
caffeinated drink they have,
feel your eyes widen as you
take your first sip.
go home, start the book you
haven't been able to get
around to. light a candle,
watch the wick slowly burn
into a pile of ash floating on
hot, vanilla scented wax.
stay up until the sun peeks
over the horizon,
realize you've been reading
the same book for six
hours straight. wipe sleep
out of your eyes. brush the
drapes to the side, open the window,
smell the air thick with moisture.
go to a coffee shop in the early morning,
right as they start to open.

you should be
your most important project.

salt water
brushes my cheek
and for once
i am beaming
like the sun.

the windows are tinted
with a thick layer of fog
as your fingers wrap around
the curls that fall across my face
and down my bare shoulders.
i am both enrobed with your warmth
and chilled by your intensity
as your palm finds the small of my back
and pulls me closer still.
yet for some reason i feel
that we are not close enough.

it's hard to open your heart
to a world that is so full
of words made to hate and
minds full of spite and jealousy
but once you are able to find a place
in which you feel embraced with love,
do not waste your opportunity.
take advantage of the light you find,
because things can turn to black
in the time it takes to draw in
an awestruck breath.

there is something captivating
about the way your fingers on my skin
brush the places i used to hate;
the places i want to be taught how to love.

poetry feeds me.
every letter
of every word
appeases a hunger
that will never be satisfied.

this morning i woke to
a golden light shining
through my lace curtains
and enrobing the pale walls of my room
in a shade the same colour
as the sun the moment before it
dips below the horizon
and i thought that maybe
this was the world saying that
today will be just as golden.

you still haven't noticed
the way you make me burn,
how your fingers leave scorch marks
on my quivering thighs, or
the scars on the inside of my eyelids
from picturing you as i drift off to sleep.
you have started a fire inside me
that has yet to show signs of
extinguishing.

you are
        gold
                and you leave your
metallic fingerprints
                                across
                        my
                skin.
with a
        single touch
you turn me
                into a masterpiece.

it almost seems unfair for me to be so blissfully happy in a time where my life is crumbling around me. i no longer have to remind myself to smile because my cheeks are already stretched wide, showcasing my brilliant not-quite-perfect teeth and the air bubbles out from my lungs but i know that this feeling isn't real and that something somewhere along the way will knock me right back to the chilling feeling of being deafeningly alone in a world where other people make waves but i barely ripple the surface of the ocean. yet, in this moment, i find myself content and surrounded by a lull of falsehood and unrealistic joviality that i know will melt away in a matter of time. maybe i should allow myself to fade into this paradise while i have the chance.

author's note

this is my life through thoughts formed into sentences.

this is the story of how i am both shining with polish and laden with rust.

thank you for helping free me from myself.

ACKNOWLEDGEMENTS

thank you to pluto irving, who has proven that i can do what i set my mind to, no matter how small i am.

thank you to anika olsen-neill, who reminds me that no matter what i do, i am never alone.

thank you to noah pacheco, for proving to me that you can do whatever it is you dream of doing.

thank you to amina chadda, for being my one-woman cheerleading squad.

thank you to nour, for the exceptional ways she contributed to the creation of this book.

thank you to lovers who shaped me, the family who raised me and the friends who supported me through and through.

a series of pinched nerves
and overworked muscles
tired of carrying a body
laden with rust;
take it, throw it in the river.
i don't have need for it anymore.

Made in the USA
Middletown, DE
07 January 2020